SCARLET

BY SAM H. FREEMAN

SERVING THEATRE

S F

SINCE 1830

SAMUELFRENCH-LONDON.CO.UK
SAMUELFRENCH.COM

Theatre Renegade is a UK based theatre company that places story, engagement and empathy at the heart of the theatrical experience. With a strong focus on new writing and social issues, we also mould and reimagine classic pieces to produce distinctive and unique adaptations.

We are a platform for new work, aiming to forge and build new creative partnerships between writers and directors whilst nurturing them from the very earliest drafts through to realised performance and print. All of our work is based upon the fundamental elements of collaboration and innovation.

Cast

Lucy Kilpatrick

Lucy trained at East 15.

Theatre includes: *Cross Purpose* (Crypt Gallery), *Merchant of Venice* (Malachite Theatre), *Courting Drama* (Bush), *The Railway Children* (Theatre by The Lake), *Let Newton Be!* (Menagerie Theatre) and *The Magpies The Wolves* (Tristan Bates).

Television includes: *Call The Midwife* (BBC).

Jade Ogugua

Jade trained at Drama Centre, London.

Television includes: *Casualty* (BBC), *Doctors* (BBC) and *The Guilty* (ITV).

Heida Reed

Heida trained at Drama Centre, London.

Theatre includes: *Macbeth* (Iris Theatre) and *Top Girls* (Out of Joint, Trafalgar Studios).

Television includes: *DCI Banks* (ITV), *Jo* (FOX), *Silent Witness* (BBC), *The Cliff* (RUV) and *Poldark* (BBC).

Asha Reid

Asha trained at East 15.

Theatre includes: *Electra* (Old Vic), *Cross Purpose* (Crypt Gallery), *Medea* (London Theatre New Cross), *Hate Play* (Box Clever), *Miniaturists: The Interval* (Arcola), *Courting Drama* (Bush Theatre), *The Magpies The Wolves* (Pleasamce/Tristan Bates), *The Lord of the Flies* (Catford Broadway), *The Tempest* (Watford Palace), *Hacked* (Theatre503) and *The Beggar's Opera* (Regent's Park Open Air).

Film includes: *Weird Love*, *Household*, *Gemma's Wedding*, *Puzzled* and *White Collar*.

Creative Team

Joe Hufton (Director)

Joe trained at LAMDA.

His most recent work includes Performance Director on *Secret Cinema* presents *Back To The Future*, the largest immersive show ever staged in the UK. In addition he also directed *Dead Poets Society* for *Secret Cinema*. He is currently working as Associate Artist on *Alice's Adventures Underground* at The Vaults (Les Enfants Terribles). Joe was Associate Artist for the international award winning Belt Up Theatre, for whom he directed *Outland* and *A Little Princess* (which both toured internationally) as well as working in association with Punchdrunk. His other recent work includes *Babylon* (National Tour) and *The Bridge That Tom Built* (for The Flanagan Collective).

Chi-San Howard (Associate/Movement Director)

Chi-San trained as a Movement Director at the Royal Central School of Speech and Drama.

Previous work includes: *The Best Pies in London* (Shakespeare in Shoreditch Festival, RIFT), *Little Red Riding Hood* (Trinity Theatre), *The Sandwich Shop* (Theatre Delicatessan), *Hansel & Gretel* (Trinity), *Schumpeter's Gale* (Rose Theatre, Kingston). She also worked as performer and choreographer for *Belt Up Theatre*.

Chi-San is co-Artistic Director of *Youaremine* who are Artists in Development at *Theatre Delicatessen*.

Sam H. Freeman (Playwright)

Sam has been part of the Lyric and Royal Court Young Writers programmes.

He has contributed short plays to *Courting Drama* (Bush Theatre and Southwark Playhouse). Other short plays include *Rules* (Theatre503), *Princess of Pop: An Extremely Fictional Account of the Britney/Christina Feud* (The Vaults), and *Career Night* (Oval House Theatre). His play *All Those Wrong Places* was the recipient of the Lost One Act award. *Scarlet* is his first full length play.

Lydia Denno (Costume and Set Designer)

Theatre includes: *Puss in Boots* (Tongue Tied Theatre), *Love Beyond* (Wembley Arena), *Wind in the Willows* (York Theatre Royal), *Bird* (Forward Theatre Project) *Boys, Fast Labour, Before the Party* (LAMDA Linbury), *Beauty and the Beast* (Engine House Theatre), *Cinderella* (Tongue Tied), *The Walworth Farce, Women of Troy, But Not As We Know It, Have a Nice Life* (LAMDA Linbury), *Conversations Not Fit for the American Dinner Table* (Tongue Tied Theatre), *Return to the Forbidden Planet* (The Castle), *The Space Between Us* (Open Clasp), *The Loneliness of the Long Distance Runner* (Pilot Theatre), *Scarberia* (Forward Theatre Project), *Blackbird* (York Theatre Royal and The Tron), *Séance on a Sunday Afternoon* (Lakeside Arts Centre), *Coram Boy* (York Theatre Royal), *Hansel and Gretel* (York Theatre Royal), *Catcher* (York Theatre Royal and Pilot Theatre), *Terrorism* (York Theatre Royal), *Me and me Dad* (Hull Truck), *Equus* (York Theatre Royal), *The White Crow* (York Theatre Royal), *Pericles* (York Theatre Royal), *I Want that Hair* (York Theatre Royal) and Assistant Designer on *The Railway Children* (York Railway Museum).

Matt Leventhall (Lighting Designer)

Matt trained at the Royal Academy of Dramatic Art and recently returned to RADA to take up post as Assistant Head of Lighting.

Theatre/Opera includes: *A Christmas Carol* (Old Red Lion), Sikes and Nancy (UK Tour and Trafalgar Studios), *Light* (Barbican and European Tour), *Mrs Warren's Profession* (John Gielgud Theatre), *Suffolk Stories* (Theatre Royal, Bury St Emunds), *God's Own Country* (UK Tour), *Bear* (Old Red Lion), *Who Framed Roger Rabbit?* (Secret Cinema), *Random* (John Gielgud Theatre), *Fishskin Trousers* (Finborough Theatre – Offie Finalist for Best Lighting Designer), *Hamlet* (St Mary's Theatre), *Bedbound* (Trinity Theatre), *The Infant* (Vivien Cox Theatre), *Bed* (Nottingham Lakeside) and *Madame Butterfly* (Leatherhead Theatre).

Conferences/Concerts include: *TEDx London* (The Roundhouse), *The Songs of My Life* (Garrick Theatre), *Plug in The Lead* (Leicester Square Theatre) and *Collaborations* (St James Theatre).

Upcoming projects in 2015 include: *Light* (Transfer to BAC), *Islands* (New Diorama and Underbelly), *Divas* (Rose Theatre and Pleasance) and *Lady Anna All At Sea* (Park Theatre).

Ed Burgon and Benji Huntrods (Composers)

Ed and Benji have collaborated on a number of film and theatre projects over the last few years including: *Indian Summer, Mirth Machine, The Midnight Oil* and several comedy sketch shows.

Ed holds two music degrees and is also involved in a number of electronic music projects.

Benji is a composer, live musician and musical director currently working under major labels with international airplay and distribution.

Katie Thackeray (Stage Manager)

Katie trained at the Guildhall School of Music and Drama.

Katie has recently worked as Deputy Stage Manager on *Norma* at Opera Holland Park, Senior Stage Manager on *Secret Cinema 21: Miller's Crossing*, Stage Manager on *Dead Poet's Society* and *Back to the Future* and Assistant Stage Manager on *The Musketeers* for Future Cinema, Company Stage Manager on *Putting it Together* at the St James and *A Little Night Music* at the Palace Theatre. Upcoming engagements include her return to Opera Holland Park as Stage Manager for their new production of *Flight*.

Brice Stratford (Fight Director)

As a Fight Director Brice's background is varied. A martial artist from a young age, he combined this with stunt training, sword fighting and a drama school education, all of which soon dragged him along the path of Fight Direction. His approach combines instinctual physical interaction and response, with technically pre-conceived choreography, allowing the focus to remain on storytelling and character expression through the medium of Fight. Amongst others, Brice has worked with the Royal National Theatre, Old Vic New Voices, Shunt, Punchdrunk, Secret Cinema, Shakespeare's Globe, Channel 4, and the BBC. He also works as an actor and director, and runs the Owle Schreame theatre company (specialising in historical performance research) and the Owle Schreame Awards (for innovation in classical theatre).

George Bach (Production Electrician)

George trained at the Royal Academy of Dramatic Art.

Production Electrician credits include: Three operas for the English Touring Opera Spring Season 2015 (Hackney Empire), *High Society* (Vanbrugh Theatre) and *Mad To Go* (GBS

Theatre) and Chief Electrician at Pleasance One, Edinburgh for the 2014 Fringe Festival.

Lighting design credits include: *Storm In A Teacup* (Soho Theatre and UK Tour), *Resolution* (Etcetera Theatre), *The Dumb Waiter* and *The Mountain Bluebird* (Courtyard Theatre) *Dogs Barking* (GBS Theatre), *Cabaret* (Nuffield Theatre), *The Wind In The Willows, The Musical* (UK Tour) and *Suffolk Stories* (Theatre Royal, Bury St Edmunds) as Re-Lighter. Upcoming projects include Lighting Designer for *The Flannelettes* at The King's Head Theatre – May 2015.

Harry Butcher (Production Sound)

Harry trained at Royal Academy of Dramatic Art.

Recent Designs: *Kill Me Now* (Associate, Park Theatre); *Miracle on 34th street* (UK tour); *The Altar Boyz* (Greenwich Theatre); *Everyday Everyday* (Associate, National Centre for Circus Arts); *The Daughter-in-Law* (GBS Theatre); *Where The Shot Rabbits Lay* (White Bear Theatre); *'New Electric Ballroom'* (GBS Theatre).

Theatrical Credits: Production Engineer, *Lippy* (UK tour); Sound No1, *Cat In The Hat* (UK tour); Sound Engineer, **Oh What A Lovely War** (UK Tour); Sound Engineer, *Taken at Midnight* (Haymarket Theatre); Sound Engineer, *Anything Can Happen* (St James Theatre); Sound Dep, *Thriller Live* (Lyric Theatre); Production Engineer, MA Director Showcase (GBS Theatre); Production Engineer, *High Society* (Vanbrugh Theatre); Sound Engineer, *See How They Run* (UK Tour).

For Theatre Renegade

Ryan Forde Iosco (Artistic Director)

Ryan trained at the Royal Central School of Speech and Drama.

He teaches in several drama schools in London and has worked with companies and theatres such as the BBC, Tanztheater Wuppertal Pina Bausch, Arcola Theatre, Universal Pictures, Sadler's Wells, Theatre503, the Soho Theatre, Compagnie DCA – Philippe Decouflé, Bush Theatre, Belt Up Theatre and Universal Pictures.

Lauren Brown (Creative Producer)

Lauren trained at the Royal Welsh College of Music and Drama.

She has worked on productions across the UK and Europe with venues including: the Bush Theatre, Southwark Playhouse, Theatre503, Queens Theatre Hornchurch and the BBC.

James Huntrods (Dramaturg)

James trained at the Royal Central School of Speech and Drama.

He has worked with theatres and production companies across the UK and abroad including: Big Talk Productions, Ovalhouse, the Soho Theatre and the Arcola Theatre.

Theatre Renegade has partnered on this production with the White Ribbon Campaign, the largest effort in the world of men working to end men's violence against women.

www.whiteribboncampaign.co.uk

@MenAntiViolence
www.whiteribboncampaign.co.uk

To wear a white ribbon is to pledge **never to commit, excuse or remain silent about violence towards women and challenge the negative gender stereotypes that underpin abuse.**

What is the White Ribbon Campaign?

The WRC is the largest effort in the world of men working to end men's violence against women. It relies on volunteer support and financial contributions from individuals and organisations.

White Ribbon Day

The International Day for the Eradication of Violence Against Women (Also known as 'White Ribbon Day') is on the 25th November. Each year, we urge men and boys to wear a ribbon for two weeks as well as encouraging men to talk in schools, workplaces, and places of worship about the problem of male violence.

We also encourage others to support the campaign by raising awareness of our cause and engaging in fundraising activities.

Get Involved

With your support, we can increase our outreach to schools and youth groups, work with unions and companies, respond to the issues of the day, and work with all communities to develop materials.

Southwark Playhouse is all about telling stories and inspiring the next generation of storytellers and theatre makers. It aims to facilitate the work of new and emerging theatre practitioners from early in their creative lives to the start of their professional careers.

Through our schools work we aim to introduce local people at a young age to the possibilities of great drama and the benefits of using theatre skills to facilitate learning. Each year we engage with over 5,000 school pupils through free schools performances and long-term in school curriculum support.

Through our Young Company (YoCo), a youth-led theatre company for local people between the ages of 14-25, we aim to introduce young people to the many and varied disciplines of running a semi-professional theatre company. YoCo provides a training ground to build confidence and inspire young people towards a career in the arts.

Our theatre programme aims to facilitate and showcase the work of some of the UK's best up and coming talent with a focus on reinterpreting classic plays and contemporary plays of note. Our two atmospheric theatre spaces enable us to offer theatre artists and companies the opportunity to present their first fully realised productions. Over the past 20 years we have produced and presented early productions by many aspiring theatre practitioners many of whom are now enjoying flourishing careers.

For more information about our forthcoming season and to book tickets visit **www.southwarkplayhouse.co.uk.** You can also support us online by joining our Facebook and Twitter pages.

Staff List

Patrons: Sir Michael Caine, Peter Gill OBE, Simon Hughes MP, Andy Serkis

Board of Trustees: Tim Wood, Sarah Hickson, Kathleen Miles, Joe Roberts, Giles Semper, Kathryn Serkis, Glenn Wellman

Artistic Director (CEO) Chris Smyrnios

General Manager Alys Mayer

Youth & Community Director David Workman

Sales & Marketing Manager Katie Walker

Press & PR Manager Susie Safavi

Technical & Production Manager Richard Seary

Production Assistant Lee Elston

House Manager Nathan Palmer

Theatre Assistant Natasha Green

Duty Managers Mark Bromley, Imogen Watson, James York

Associate Director David Mercatali

Scarlet

by Sam H. Freeman

ISBN 978-0-573-11169-3

www.samuelfrench-london.co.uk www.samuelfrench.com

Cover image by Kunal Verma

For Isabel Hickey

Who believed you should be who you are.

Special thanks to Zoe Anuji-Robinson, Kristen Atherton,
Diana Atuona, Nicola Bland, Lauren Brown, Oliver
Dawe, Maureen Freeman, Steve Freeman, Francis Grin,
Stephen Hudson, Joe Hufton, Adam Hughes,
James Huntrods, Ryan Forde Iosco, Lucy Kilpatrick,
Eleanor Lawrence, Chris MacDonald, Sarah Milton,
Alice Northey, Jade Ogugua, Heida Reed, Asha Reid,
Anna Tierney, Hannah Warren-Green, Ben Weatherill.

1

4 women on stage. They are all Scarlet.

Scarlet sometimes plays other characters from the story. When she does so, she does not become them, only acts them. Therefore her interpretations may be biased.

A '/' indicates a point where the next line overlaps

Bold lines indicate where the Scarlets are recreating scenes from the story, or things that other characters said.

The lines attributions are suggestions; in line with the original production. The director should feel free to move them around if s/he feels it helps their vision of the story.

1 The first person I ever had sex with was Alex.

4 Well, I say Alex, his name was actually Sean,

1 but I didn't realise this till two weeks later when he friend requested me.

3 Our mate was having a birthday party at a church hall in Brockley; we did it in the disabled loo.

2 I know, classy,

1 but where else were we meant to go? We were fourteen, and wasted.

2 My overriding memory of the experience is that, strangely,

1 I rather enjoyed it. After Alex there was Peter, John, Theo,

4 Robin,

3 Neil, Omar,

2 Harry,

1 Lewis,

3 Theresa,

2 and Emilio.

 Beat.

1 The first person to ever make me come was Freddy.

2 Freddy was an American piano prodigy; as in, a piano prodigy from America, not a prodigy of specifically the American Piano. He was also my friend's cousin, and she was not best pleased about it all.

3 "All right! It's not like he's your brother! You've only met him twice in your life!"

1 (I actually did have sex with her brother one time, but that's a whole other thing)

3 It was Freddy's tongue, not his fingers, that... um... well, it was very long.

1 Oh boy.

2 After Freddy there was

1 Ashley, Trev, Roland, Rory... That other one,

4 The one with the hair,

1 That other other one,

2 Irish,

3 and Psycho Sam who could only get it up if the radio was tuned into Choice FM.

2 I often wonder about his childhood.

 Beat.

4 The first person to tell me they loved me, (apart from my mum), was Daniel. We'd only known each other two weeks. I remember wondering if this was an indicator of mental instability.

2 A skeleton in the closet.

1 A hidden defect.

3 Faulty goods.

4 It's not that I didn't feel it too. It's just that I thought you were meant to wait a while before actually saying it.

3 I wasn't sure that I could return it without cringing, so I took a gamble and went for a

    2 picks out 1 to be Daniel. She throws her arms around his neck and kisses him.

3 We met at a barbecue in Manchester, towards the end of second year.

    Suddenly we're at the barbecue. Daniel working up the courage to approach Scarlet.

    He opened with

1/**DANIEL** **We're um, we're not really at a barbecue, y'know.**

    The rest of the Scarlets look around, confused.

2 **Oh, really? I'm imagining this then?**

1/**DANIEL** **Not a barbe–**

3 He actually has a slight Welsh accent,

1 but I can't do it, so I won't try.

4 It's not important to the story.

1/**DANIEL** **Not a barbecue, this. Barbecuing is slow cooking with indirect heat. Technically, what they're doing here is grilling. This is a grill.**

3 Oh, I see, this is like, weird flirting. And yet, strangely, it's kind of working. I'm going to be honest with you, I think it's mainly because he's

2 FUCKING HOT.

3 This is the first time I've met him, but I've seen him out in town a few times before, always with a gaggle of women basically hanging off of him. Let's face it, it's not for the quality of his chat. He looks like a slightly manlier Justin Bieber,

4 and before you're all like "Ew, what?"…

3 Come on, be honest with yourself. You would.

1/DANIEL **I'm Daniel.**

2 **Scarlet.**

1/DANIEL **Who do you know here then?**

2 **I live with Sasha? She's a friend of Scott's.**

1/DANIEL **Ah okay, I know Scott. Top lad, top lad.**

2 **Not enjoying the food then?**

1/DANIEL **It's not that; it's just that, if I go to a barbecue, I hope there'll actually be some barbecue.**

2 **Maybe you should pop out, get a cheeky pizza or something?**

1/DANIEL **Maybe I should. If I do, will you go with me? So I look like less of a dick?**

2 **Not really hungry.**

Beat.

1/DANIEL **Oh.**

SCARLET *tries not to laugh.*

2 **Tell you what, how about we stick around for a while, see how we feel later?**

3 Three hours on, I'm sat opposite him in Pizza Hot One, sharing a fifteen inch vegetable supreme. Turns out he's quite a decent conversationalist. I've since realised that he just gets a bit tongue tied around new people. Which actually, is quite cute.

4 The first person I ever said the words 'I love you' to, (apart from my mum), was Daniel.

   DANIEL *and* **SCARLET** *are lying on a sofa in the dark, illuminated solely by the light of the television they are watching.*

   I was about five weeks behind him. We were lying on his sofa one night, watching some panel show. It'd been playing on my mind all evening, just out of nowhere. Something about the way he chopped the garlic for our dinner. So I just did it, I just said the words so that they were out there and it was done.

3 **I love you.**

1/**DANIEL** **Bout time.**

4 And then we went back to the telly and nothing more was said.

   Beat. The scene comes apart.

3 The first person who ever completely and utterly fucked the shit out of my life was Will Brooks.

1 And I guess this is where the story begins, really. Will was a guy who lived in the same halls as me back in first year, although I didn't ever speak to him back then. The first time I properly met Will was one evening around the middle of second year, a little bit before I started seeing Daniel. I'd been meant to be meeting Sasha at the student union for a few drinks, but she'd had to cancel. I'd decided to go along anyway; I was in one of those moods. I had an itch to scratch.

We're in the student union. **SCARLET** *is sat at the bar.*
WILL *approaches her, being egged on by his mates.*

4/WILL **Alright?**

1 **Hi.**

4/WILL **How's it going?**

1 **Yeah, not bad. You?**

4/WILL **Yeah. Um. Yeah. Not bad... either.**

Awkward silence. **WILL** *looks back, his mates urge him on.*

Can I buy you a drink?

SCARLET *holds up her pint.*

1 **Got one already.**

4/WILL **Oh yeah.**

WILL's *mates laugh.*

1 I can't imagine Will has much luck with the ladies. His
face, okay this is going to sound harsh but I'm just
trying to describe him to you, his face looks a little bit
like he might be inbred. And he smells like a farm. I'm
pretty sure the joke must be on him. And so, because
I like to think of myself as a nice person, and because
every time I see Will I think of how in first year he
stayed in halls, on his own, over Christmas, I say:

Doesn't mean you can't buy yourself one though.

WILL *smiles, relieved. He takes a seat next to* **SCARLET**.
One of the other **SCARLETS** *hands him a pint. Awkward silence.*

**So, uh, Will, what's your um, your, what do you what
do you... study?**

The conversation carries on in much this fashion. It's not that he isn't making an effort, I think he's making a lot of effort, it just *looks* like he isn't. Aware that we are being watched, I try to make it look like we're having a great time. I smile a lot, and laugh when I think he's trying to be funny. A nice, friendly laugh that very clearly says

"I like you, I respect you, but I do not necessarily want to have sex with you."

A lot of people mix that one up with something else, so it's important to be specific. And once I think I've given him a decent amount of time...

Right. I have to go.

4/WILL **What?**

1 **I'm meeting a mate in twenty minutes. But it was really really nice to finally meet you.**

4/WILL **Stay for another.**

1 **Sorry, I'm running late.**

4/WILL **Get your mate to come down here.**

1 **I can't.**

> SCARLET *starts to gather her stuff.* WILL *glances back to where his mates are – a bit of panic.* SCARLET *gets her coat on.*

4/WILL **Which way you heading?**

1 **Uh, just into town.**

4/WILL **Oh cool. I gotta go that way soon anyway. Might come with you.**

> *Beat.*

1 **Okay.**

4/WILL **Yeah, just. Might as well have company.**

1 **No of course.**

> **WILL** *offers his arm, and she (politely) takes it. The boys cheer.*

> It's clear what's going on. I have two options: Either I march up to them and inform them that we are not leaving together, or I let it go.

> *Beat. She considers.*

> Oh fuck it. I can't quite bare to embarrass him that badly. What do I care?

> *He gathers his stuff and they leave.*

3/SASHA **Scar, did you have sex with Will Brooks last night?**

> **SASHA** *is eating a sandwich.* **SCARLET** *has a Sainsbury's bag with her lunch in it.*

2 I meet Sasha in town the next day for lunch.

> **Oh my god, no.**

3/SASHA **He's telling everyone you did. Said after you were at union.**

2 **What? No, I just had a drink with him.**

3/SASHA **I've heard it from LITERALLY about a hundred people.**

> **SCARLET** *takes this in.*

2 **What a prick…**

3/SASHA **So you really didn't?**

2 **Sash, please, give me some credit.**

3/SASHA **Never know with you babes. What you gonna do?**

2 **I don't know.**

3/SASHA **Scar, you can't let people get away with spreading shit about you. He's probably saying you're a right dirty minge.**

SCARLET *is unsure.*

3/SASHA **You know what? Leave it to me.**

2 **Sash…**

3/SASHA **You think no one liked him before? Just wait till I'm finished. I am texting *everyone*.**

2 And she does (text everyone). Sasha's got so many contacts she had to buy an extra phone, and she loves a bit of drama. Before I've finished half a sandwich, there isn't a person on campus who doesn't know that Will Brooks is a desperate pervert with a bad BO problem and a

3/SASHA *(texting from two phones at once)* **tincey… (How d'ya spell tincey? Nevermind)… tin… cey… nee… dle… dick. SEND.**

She sends the texts.

I've really outdone myself this time. He might have to transfer…

2 The texts cause a bit of a stir. In the hour following, Sasha's phone barely stops vibrating. Everyone wants in on the joke. She continues to forward me responses all afternoon; messages and pictures and screenshots of Whatsapp conversations. It starts to feel a bit cruel. The following day, I overhear two girls I've never even met discussing it in the library. The librarian has to tell them off for giggling too loud.

Beat.

Next time I see Will is a few weeks later.

WILL *appears, looking hateful.*

I pass him in a corridor. He's with a group of his mates, and they jostle him when they see me. They're laughing at him. The look he shoots me is pure hatred. I feel bad for him but... You reap what you sow. Not my fault.

Beat.

3　Two weeks later, I meet Daniel. Eight months later, I'm all loved up. It's horrible! I'm really worried that I've become one of those people I promised myself I wouldn't; the type that says things like

1　"Hun, tell you what, we need to find you a boyfriend!"

4　"Oh I'd love to, but Dan and I thought we'd have a night in."

3　or, the absolute worst,

1, 2, AND 4　"When you know, you just know."

3　I mean, I've never actually said that, but one time I caught myself thinking it, and well...

1　Tonight, I am going to a party!

2　And, in an effort to convince the world that I am still the coolest sista in town, it is a different party to one that Daniel is going to.

4　(Also because I think Sasha might disown me if I don't go with her.)

Knock on the door.

3/SASHA　**Oi! Are you ready yet?**

1　**Just about.**

SASHA *comes in. Looks* **SCARLET** *up and down.*

3/SASHA　**Uh, really?**

1　**What?**

3/SASHA **You have a boyfriend.**

1 **So what, suddenly I'm a nun?**

SASHA *isn't convinced.*

3/SASHA **Just, don't talk to Ben.**

1 **Ugh, not this again.**

3/SASHA **He'll spend the whole time staring at your legs!**

1 **Sash, for the last time, you have lovely legs!**

3/SASHA **I have NO legs! I have bum, and then feet!**

1 **Bullshit.**

3/SASHA **Fine. Whatever. Meet me downstairs, I'm prinking.**

2 (Pre-drinking.)

They all down shots and then...

PARTY!

Blackout.

–

Lights up. SCARLET*'s room. Hungover to death.*

4 I'm lying on top of my bed.

1 I'm still in my party clothes.

2 Light is pouring in through the blinds.

3 I've been sick on the floor.

Beat.

1 It's funny because I had about three drinks...

2 Then again I only remember about an hour of the night so...

3 **Ow ow ow ow ow ow ow.**

4 That's me trying to sit up.

   3 *throws up.*

2 Time time time what's the time?

1 Oh god I have not felt like this in quite a while.

2 I want to shout to Sash for some water, but I think if I speak my head might explode.

4 It's one pm.

ALL Shit.

   SASHA *calls.* **SCARLET** *finds her phone and answers.*

3/SASHA **Um. Scar?**

4 **Oh my god... my head feels like someone replaced my brain with broken glass.**

3/SASHA **Have you seen Facebook?**

4 **What?**

3/SASHA **You should probably have a look. Will Brooks tagged you in a video.**

4 **For fuck's sake, what did I do?**

3/SASHA **It already has five likes, and a comment from someone called Jed Towler!? It says "What a slag."**

4 **What is this?**

3/SASHA **You should probably just have a look.**

2 I press play.

   It is important that we can see the video, and it has been made to look real. It's been filmed on a camera-phone. In it, a completely out-of-it **SCARLET** *sits on a bed, while various boys goad her and ask her questions. Sometimes they touch her inappropriately. She giggles through most* *of it, as if she thinks they're all just having some good banter, and this governs the way she responds to every question – as if it's all a bit of fun. She is BEYOND DRUNK.*

SUGGESTIONS

The content of the video should be ad-libbed and improvised, to give it the feeling of being busy and drunken and out-of-control. **SCARLET** *probably doesn't respond to everything, as it is all going on at the same time.*

The content of the video should be as horrible and disturbing as you can bare to make it.

Some questions that might be asked are:

"How many boys have you fucked?" – **SCARLET** *thinks around 30. The boys think this is a lot.*

"Have you fucked anyone in this room?" – She doesn't know. She probably looks around, but, in her state, can't see that well.

"Name all the men you've fucked" – She can't remember all the names – she might try and name some and then start drawing blanks, or she may just say she can't remember them all.

"Why are you such a slut?" – **SCARLET** *probably tells whoever asked to "Fuck off", but in a light-hearted way. She thinks she's in on the joke.*

"Show us your tits." **SCARLET** *won't do this, and so one boy tries to pull her top down. She slaps his hand away, but he manages to get a good feel. This may get a cheer or two from the others.*

Other statements might be thrown in:

One boy asserts that she gave his mate at STD (crabs?)

*One boy asks why anyone would bother; "she must be
loose as a bargain bucket" or "there's no way you'd touch
the sides."*

"She probably stinks man."

*Maybe someone/a few guys chant Get Your Rat Out For
The Lads.*

*We do not see all of the video, only a segment. We return
to* **SCARLET**.

2 It goes on for about ten minutes.

1 I name boys I've slept with and talk about big dicks and
   favourite positions. At one point the camera looks up
   my skirt.

4 Somehow, I'm not wearing any underwear.

3/SASHA **Babe, are you alright?**

4 **Um, not really, no. Excuse me.**

   SCARLET *heads back up to her room, phone in hand.*

   I stare at the screen for a full minute, trying to decide
   if I should write something. But I – No I –

   Beat.

   I send a message to Will. "Please, please you need to
   take it down it's not funny."

2 'Seen'.

4 'Will you need to fucking take it down now I swear'.

2 Seen.

4 'WILL'.

2 Seen.

4   Oh my god. Two shares. Two people have shared this.

    SCARLET's phone starts ringing. She looks at it.

    It's Daniel.

    She doesn't pick up.

    It keeps ringing.

    She answers.

4   **Hello?**

1/DANIEL   **Ello ello.**

4   **Hi.**

1/DANIEL   **You feeling rough? You even up yet?**

    Beat.

4   **Yeah.**

1/DANIEL   **You don't sound it.**

    Beat.

    Scarlet?

4   **Yeah?**

1/DANIEL   **Listen, I'm in your area. Fancy getting some lunch?**

4   **Um. I feel a bit sick.**

1/DANIEL   **I thought you weren't going to hit it hard?**

4   **I'll call you back.**

    She hangs up. Winces. Stares at the phone. She is holding back the panic.

3   Call him back. Just call him back.

2   No. Hang on.

3 You've got nothing to/ hide you did nothing wrong.

2 No hang on, hang on, just think about it –

    4 *calls him back, unable to hold back the tide.*

    2 *is frustrated.*

1/DANIEL **Hi, what's up?**

    Beat.

    Scar?

4 You need to check Facebook.

1/DANIEL **What?**

    She is now hysterical.

4 **On Will Brook's profile. I don't remember it I don't remember any of it.**

1/DANIEL **What are you talking about?**

4 **There's this video and they made me say things and now they won't take it down.**

1/DANIEL **Okay. Hang on. Hang on. I'll call you back.**

    He hangs up. She puts her phone on the ground and steps away from it. They all watch it, waiting for him to call back. A long pause.

    SCARLET*'s phone rings. She looks at it.*

3 It's three hours later. I've called him back thirty two times with no response.

    SCARLET *picks up.*

    Hello?

2/AMANDA **Scarlet hunny, it's Amanda.**

4 Dan's housemate.

2/AMANDA Um, so, Dan's here with me. He got into a fight.

4 What? Is he okay?

2/AMANDA He'll be fine. Nothing life threatening; just a bit black and blue.

4 Who'd he get into a fight with?

2/AMANDA Will Brooks.

Beat. **SCARLET** *grimaces.*

4 Okay, I'm on my way.

She goes to **DANIEL***'s house.*

4 Daniel does not look good at all. Swollen eyes, split lips, all the colours of the rainbow.

1/DANIEL It's alright, I managed to get a few punches in. Then his mates jumped me.

4 I can't believe you did that.

1/DANIEL I almost bought a knife. I almost bought a fucking knife.

4 Are you okay?

1/DANIEL Have you reported the video?

4 Yes.

1/DANIEL Have they taken it down?

4 I don't know. They hadn't when I left.

1/DANIEL Well, you need to check. And then call them or something. You need to get it taken off.

4 Okay, I will. Are you okay?

1/DANIEL I'm fine. Go get my laptop, it's in my room.

4 I'd really like a hug, if that's okay?

1/DANIEL Sorry, of course you would. Sorry. Come here.

SCARLET *hugs him. She has to be careful, as she doesn't want to hurt him.*

Don't worry, it's gonna be fine. We'll sort it out.

3   He sounds confident, but I don't think he is. There's no sleep to be had that night; we lie in bed, both completely aware of each other's insomnia, but staying silent.

1/DANIEL **Scar?**

Silence.

4 **Yeah?**

Silence.

1/DANIEL **How many guys have you... y'know... been with?**

Silence.

4 **Uh... don't know. Never really counted.**

Silence.

Why?

1/DANIEL **Just not something we've ever talked about.**

Silence.

4 **What about you?**

Silence.

1/DANIEL **Uh... yeah, no, same. Never counted.**

Silence.

2 It takes three days for the video to be taken down; in that time, the views and shares continue to spiral. There's a strange atmosphere in my lecture on Monday morning, and I know. They've all seen it. Boys shout things at me as I walk across campus. Eyes follow me

down corridors. And then there are the GIFs. Some
lovely person has taken still images from the video and
animated them together. Apparently they're hilarious.

Beat.

For my part, I'm taking it all with my head held high.
Not even flinching. In the grand scheme of things, it's
an embarrassing moment. A cruel joke played by a sad,
bitter boy. And if I react, I give him what he wants.
Everyone will have moved on to something else in a
month. It's Dan that I feel bad for, actually. I mean, he
doesn't mention it, to protect me, but one time I saw a
group of lads heckle him. I feel responsible.

3/SASHA **You have to be careful babes. With boys like Will
Brooks.**

1 **So what, this is my fault?**

3/SASHA **No I'm not saying it's anyone's fault –**

1 **It is. It's his fault.**

3/SASHA **No, obviously, yeah.**

1 **It's his fault, Sash.**

Beat.

3/SASHA **You do get very drunk though.**

1 **And?**

3/SASHA **I'm just being a mate Scar.**

1 **Well then support me.**

3/SASHA **I am. I'm giving you advice. You get wasted/**

1 **/As do you.**

3/SASHA **and you behave in a certain way, and you dress
quite… y'know, and it… it gives off… an impression.**

1 **What, 'assault me'?**

3/SASHA You have slept around quite a lot.

1 Oh fuck you.

   Pause.

3/SASHA I'm not trying to be a bitch, I'm really not. And
   I'm not blaming you. I'm just saying that boys... do
   this kind of thing. That's just life. And it's shit but...
   you've gotta look after yourself.

1 I bet you're loving this.

3/SASHA What?

1 "Well, you did fuck half the campus Scarlet so what do
   you expect?"

3/SASHA I didn't say that.

1 Well, I'm really sorry that I have a sex life and you don't
   cos you're stumpy and boss-eyed and no-one wants
   you!

4 Okay, so, a *little* bit below the belt. But you have to
   remember that I'm pissed off. She's not even really
   boss eyed. Like, a little bit, but not that much.

   SCARLET *and* **SASHA** *both storm off in different
   directions.*

   SCARLET's *phone starts to ring. She looks at it, doesn't
   recognise the number, and picks up.*

4 Hello?

2/MAN Uh, hi. Is this Scarlet?

4 Yes. Who's this?

2/MAN Um, hi, um. I was wondering if I could enquire
   about your rate?

4 I'm sorry my what?

2/MAN **Your rate. Do you charge by the hour? And do you do out-calls?**

Beat. She understands and falters. 3 *urges her to hang up, supported by* 1.

4 **Who is this?**

2/MAN **Um, no, I'm just um, I'm just in town for one night, at a hotel. I just wanted to know if –**

4 **Where did you get this number?**

2/MAN **I'm sorry I think there's been a mistake I'm really sorry really sorry I really am.**

He hangs up. She is shocked.

4 This happens three more times over the next two weeks. I manage to find out that one of them got my number from a bus stop, and the other from the inside of a toilet door. The third time, the calls comes at 2am, and Dan and I are in bed. He grabs the phone off of me and starts screaming down it. Afterwards he goes downstairs, and I hear the front door slam. He doesn't come back till the morning. That day I go and get my number changed, and that puts an end to that.

2 An embarrassing moment, nothing more.

4 The weeks go by, and I start to put it all behind me. Like I said, people get bored. No one's talking about it any more, or at least not in my hearing. Soon it will be like it never happened.

Beat.

2 It's Dan's birthday today. He doesn't want to do anything for it; he's not big on birthdays. I know, I know; believe me, I've tried to persuade him. But exam season is here, and he's been dragging his feet on this one piece of coursework for about a month now.

3 Yawn.

4 I feel like I barely see him anymore.

   Minor beat.

2 I think I might surprise him. Bake up a little romantic
   storm and take it over. Gorge ourselves on cake and
   watch an old film. Y'know, bring a bit of the magic
   back. Maybe get the baby oil out.

1 He fucking loves a bit of baby oil, Dan does. He's like an
   early Take That video.

4 I have a bit of a confession to make… I've never actually
   baked anything in my life.

3 It can't be that hard though right? Sasha's doing it all
   the time. Actually, Sasha's doing it ALL THE TIME.
   I've been considering ways to gently suggest to her that
   maybe she should start baking a bit less, and *maybe* get
   a gym membership instead, but after our little fiasco a
   few weeks ago, I think it might be a while before I can
   say something like that and not have her hate me…
   Maybe she'll figure it out for herself.

2 Anyway, I google up some recipes. 'Sexy… cakes… for…
   birthday grumps…'

3 Hmm…

4 'Gerta's All-Butter Red-Velvet Love Muffins'

1 Smutty…

2 I nip down to Tesco, pick up all the ingredients, then set
   to work!

   The **SCARLET***s bring out various cake ingredients and a
   big mixing bowl.*

4 It's an American recipe. I don't really understand the
   measurements.

3   What's the fuck is a 'cup'? What kind of cup? A mug? What size? I don't get it.

1   So I just kind of guess, and then add a bit of extra sugar, because that can never be a bad thing.

The **SCARLET***s throw various amounts of various ingredients into the bowl and MIX. Then pour in a ton of sugar. Then spray in some whipped cream.*

3   I forget to preheat the oven, so I just turn it up a bit higher.

The bowl goes away.

4   While they bake, I jump in the shower and make myself smell pretty. And twenty-five minutes later…

3   I pull from the oven a tray of what look like slightly bloody poos.

4   Oh.

3   They don't even smell nice.

4   This is not good.

1   Um.

2   Okay.

4   Bin them bin them bin them.

2   Back down to Tesco. No time for more baking so I'll just have to bring shop bought.

1   Except they don't have cupcakes in Tesco Metro, so I get 'Flapjack Bites' instead,

4   BUT, I reckon if I stick a candle in each one it will still be special. It's the thought that counts, right?

2   Back to the house.

4   Do my hair. Do my dress. I pick out his favourite one, the one that he's always like "You should wear that one."

I write him a funny little message in the birthday card
that I have HAND MADE.

3 Hell yes.

4 And wrap up his present; a little remote control car,
because he always goes on about how much he misses
those.

*Then they pick up a picnic hamper (packed with baby
oil, flapjack bites, candles, funny hand-made card, and
present) and set off.*

I have to catch a bus across town to get to Dan's. While
I wait at the stop, I think about what a warm evening
it is, and how we could maybe sit out on the balcony
outside Dan's bedroom window. The sky is red and
purple and blue and orange. It's a fifteen minute
journey, and then a ten minute walk from the bus stop
at the other end. I pick some daisies in the little park
on their road. It's this in-joke we have. And then I'm
at the door.

SCARLET *knocks. Waits. Ruffs up her hair.*

Amanda answers. She's looking a bit dressed up too.

2/AMANDA **Oh! Hey babe.**

1 **Hey.**

2/AMANDA **We weren't expecting you! Dan said you
couldn't come!**

Beat.

1 **Uh, what?**

2/AMANDA **They've all gone to the restaurant already. I'm
running late so we can go together if you don't mind
waiting a few minutes?**

1 **The restaurant?**

2/AMANDA Yeah.

1 Which restaurant?

2/AMANDA La Porchetta. The Italian on the high street.

1 Is Dan there?

2/AMANDA It's his birthday, be a bit silly if he wasn't. Sorry,
I think he thought you weren't coming. Said you had a
family thing?

Pause. **SCARLET** *can't quite believe what she's been told;
she is dumbstruck.*

You ok?

Pause.

Scarlet, you ok?

1 Yeah! Fine! Yeah, sorry. No I'm fine.

Beat.

Yeah, I have a… a family thing. But I had a bit of extra
time, so I thought I'd drop off his present.

2/AMANDA Oh. Okay. I can give it to him for you if you
want?

1 No, no, I'll do it some other time. I want to give it to him
myself. Um. I've got to go actually.

Beat.

2/AMANDA Ok.

1 Can you not tell him that I came? I just think otherwise
he'll be disappointed.

2/AMANDA Um. Yeah if you want?

SCARLET *leaves.*

I hope everything's alright!

SCARLET climbs into bed.

1 The first time someone I love ever made me cry was…

3 it was right now.

2 I go home and I climb into bed and I sob into my
   flapjack bites.

4 And I wonder if maybe I'm being punished?

   –

   Time has passed.

2 As far as I know, Amanda never mentions to Dan my
   appearance at his birthday event. And I never mention
   it to him. It's been quite an intense month for
   both of us, and maybe I just need to accept that he
   needed some time without me. That's what you do in
   relationships isn't it? You accept people's flaws.

3 But the thing is, it never really gets back to normal.

4 I feel like I'm seeing less and less of him. We never stay
   at his any more; we always go back to mine.

1 He rarely wants to have sex,

4 and when he does, it's… different.

1 He used to be all about the eye contact. He would really
   stare you in the eyes during sex. It used to freak me
   out a bit, but I miss it now that it's gone.

4 I don't think he finds me attractive anymore. I feel like
   I'm in one of those depressing indie films about a
   failing marriage.

   Beat.

3 I start picturing other people while we do it. It's like my
   secret revenge against him. I begin with just people I
   know. And then people he knows. Then his friends.
   Then his flatmates. Then one time even his dad. And

then one night I go out and I meet this guy called
Michael, who may or may not be a lecturer somewhere
in the uni, and I go back to his and have sex with him.
It's not very good and he cries after he comes and in
the morning he tells me he has a wife and that she
might be coming home so I have to get out out out.

Beat.

I call up Dan that day and tell him I think we need to
meet up for a chat. He suggests that we should just
have the conversation over the phone. I tell him that
I think we should end the relationship, and he agrees.
He says to me, on the phone, he actually says the words

1 "I wish you all the best for the future."

    Beat.

2 And then it's done. I sort of feel better,

4 but I also sort of feel much much worse.

2 I understand, I do; I get that people have relationships
   and then they break up. And it's horrible to start off
   with but then you get over it and find someone else
   and it's all okay.

4 Telling myself this doesn't help though. I literally spend
   days in bed. The only places I go are the toilet and the
   fridge.

3 Three days in, Sasha actually physically pulls me out.

4 I can't be bothered to fight, so I allow her. And then
   when she's not looking I go back.

3 I resent her. No matter how sympathetic she tries to be,
   I can't help look at her and think that inside her head
   she's saying "Let's be honest babe, you did kind of
   bring it on yourself."

4 And then one day there's a fucking disaster;

1 we run out of Cheese Strings.

3 And so I am forced out into the world in a quest for junk food.

2 And then this really weird thing happens in Costcutter. I freak out. I literally freak out because I'm convinced that everyone is staring at me. I leave the shop without buying anything and go straight home.

3 And then…

1 And then…

4 It all just…

2 spirals.

> **SCARLET** *is thrust into an exam situation. Table, chair, exam paper.*

> I'm sat in an exam, and our lecturer is starting the timer.

> *We can hear the clock ticking SO LOUDLY.* **SCARLET** *stares at the exam paper as if trying to burn a hole in it.*

> I can't make the questions make sense in my head. The more I read them, the less sense they make.

1 'The Articles of Association provide that the preference shares carry the right to a 12 per cent/ preference dividend and a prior right to the return of their capital on a winding up.'

3 'They have no right to vote except/ at class meetings. The board of directors wants to reduce the preference dividend from 12 to 8 per cent.'

4 'The company has 100,000/ £1 preference shares and 500,000 £1 ordinary shares.'

1 'Alternatively, he has suggested that the company re-registers as a private limited –'

2 *shushes all of the voices, desperately.*

2 I manage to answer one question. Badly. I'm not even sure if it's coherent; just desperate rantings on a page. With two days till my second paper, and my head in a more messy panicky place than ever, it all seems a bit hopeless.

And so I take control of the situation.

SCARLET *produces a big bottle of vodka and drinks from it.*

3 Or maybe I don't.

ALL DANIEL!

1 I'm on his doorstep, daisies in my hair, wondering if there's ever a situation where vomiting on someone's doorstep could be endearing.

4 DANIEL I LOVE YOU! DANIEL!

The front door opens, spilling light out onto her. **AMANDA** *stands at the other side.*

2/AMANDA Hun, it's one o'clock in the morning.

4 Can I speak to Daniel please?

2/AMANDA He's asleep.

4 But his light's on.

2/AMANDA He's busy.

4 DANIEL!

2/AMANDA Scarlet. Seriously.

3 He appears at the top of the stairs in his underwear, pulling a t-shirt over his head.

4 Hi.

1/DANIEL Scarlet, what the fuck?

4 I wanted to see you.

1/DANIEL I'm not your boyfriend. You can't show up here whenever.

4 I think we made a mistake.

> DANIEL, *awkwardly, does not respond.*

I just want to know what I did?

1/DANIEL You're fucking wasted.

4 *(holding out her arms for a hug)* Daniieeeeel.

1/DANIEL I'm going back to bed.

4 I will stand out here and scream ALL NIGHT LONG.

1/DANIEL Go home Scarlet.

4 DAAAAAAAANIEEEEEEEEL.

1/DANIEL What do you want me to say? What are you looking for?

> *Pause.*

I don't feel the way you want me to feel. I'm sorry, but that's all it comes down to. Would you have wanted me to go on pretending?

> *Beat. He regrets it.*

I'm sorry, that's… that wasn't very nice. I'm tired, and you're drunk. Look, I've moved on, and you need to as well.

> *She's either too drunk or too disheartened to respond.*

Scar?

> *No response.*

I'm going go back to bed. Don't do this again.

4 Can I stay with you?

1/DANIEL **No.**

2 And then he disappears back inside and shuts the door. I'm left in the dark, the only light coming down from his bedroom window. I look up to it. There's a girl staring back down at me, through the curtains.

1 It's only been two weeks.

3 It's only been two fucking weeks.

2 And then she disappears back inside too, probably to be with him.

4 I start to cry.

    4 *starts to cry.*

2 *(irritated with crying 4)* And cry, and cry. I cry REALLY LOUDLY, apparently.

4 *(trying to fight back)* I cry purposefully loudly, because I think if he has to listen to his ex-girlfriend sobbing her heart out, he might not be able to get it up.

1 And then I throw up.

2 *(irritated)* And I do that loudly too.

4 because I think it might add to the general effect.

2 *(to 4)* Get up. Come on.

4 I can't!

2 You're embarrassing yourself.

4 I'm heartbroken!

2 And this is helping?

1 *(to 2)* Leave her alone.

2 *(to 1)* Don't need your input thanks.

1 Pardon me?

2 *(to 1)* You're the last thing we need.

1 We? I'm sorry,/ who's we?

4 DANIEL.

2 *(to 4)* What do you think is going to happen? Do you think he's going- [to march down here and take you back?]

   4 *wretches.*

2 *(to 4)* You're a mess. You're a fucking mess.

1 *(to 2)* And you're an uptight bitch –   3 Hey.

2 *(to 1)* Uptight? Really/? Uptight? Maybe if we'd been a bit more –

1 *(to 2)* You're think you're/ so much better than –

2 *(to 1)* You know what you can just/ go away –

4 DAAAAAN/IIIEEEEEL.

2 *(to 4)* Oh my god. SHUT UP/. SHUT.UP. 3 Stop.

1 *(to 2)* I can't stand you, I/ actually can't –

2 *(to 1)* And I can't stand/ you.

   4 *is wailing.*

1 *(to 2)* You're so fucking /stuck-up –   3 STOP IT.

2 *(to 1)* Look at yourself. /LOOK AT –

1 *(to 2)* NO ONE LIKES YOU –

2 *(to 1)* YOU'RE A SLUT, YOU'RE A FUCKING –

   3 *screams with rage. Everyone is silenced, shocked.*

   SCARLET*'s psyche cracks.* 3 *breaks away from the others.*

3 FUCK THIS.

2 Excuse me?

3 An hour later, I'm back at the flat.

The other **SCARLET***s are confused by this.*

2　What is she doing?

　　3 *produces a suitcase.*

　　Hey.

3　A few hours after that, I'm at the train station. I buy a
　　ticket for the first train to London. Still drunk.

　　Another swig from the vodka bottle.

2　We didn't agree to this.

3　Still *really* drunk. Tickets out. Down the platform.

2　Hang on.

4　What's she…?

　　*She's out of control She produces her phone and starts
　　searching for something on it. The others are protesting,
　　but she's not listening. They handle her like a bomb that
　　might go off any second (there are suggested lines for the
　　other* **SCARLET***s, but a certain amount of ad-libbing is
　　allowed here, for the sake of creating the desired effect).*

3　Suitcase dragging. I'm on the train, and my head is
　　still spinning as I scroll down through pictures on my
　　phone.

1　/Hey, calm down.

3　Summer barbecues, nights out, my birthday…

2　Scarlet.

3　… country walks, Valentines Day…

2　Scarlet. Listen.

3　… and there they are. Five pictures, from last Christmas;
　　Dan, stood in front of a bathroom mirror, top off,
　　pants down, dick in hand.

4 No. No no no.

3 He's playing with himself and staring into the camera.

2 /You're drunk. Think about this.

3 A cheeky present to say he missed me. How sweet.

2 Stop this. Right now. Stop.

3 The train is pulling out of the station and I can't even see straight. Onto Facebook, upload pictures, tag Daniel Westcott... I try to think of a snappy title but nothing comes, so I simply caption them 'Dan Masturbating'.

2 Ok, grab the phone!

The others make to grab **3**, *but she clicks her fingers and they disappear. She is alone. She has all the power.*

3 Thanks for the memories Dan. Let's see how you like it.

She smiles, it is satisfying.

Post.

She posts the pictures.

Blackout.

End of Part One.

*1, 2 and 4 are centre stage. They have changed, their look is a lot more conservative: different hair, different make-up, different clothes. The relationship between them has also changed; whereas in the first half it felt something like a democracy, now there is a definite leader: *2*.*

4 is her right hand woman.

1 is desperate to be in the gang, but the other two don't like her very much.

3 is sat in a corner, in the dark – none of the others interact with her; they are pretending she doesn't exist. She still looks exactly how she did in the first half.

2 When Eleanor and Oliver first met, sparks flew.

4 Ellie's one of those girls; everywhere she goes, people just fall in love with her.

2 She has this effortless grace.

4 She's the classic beauty. The heroine of the story.

2 And no matter how hard you try, you can't quite bring yourself to hate her;

4 she's just so so nice.

2 They work at an exclusive member's club in Soho. Ellie's a hostess. Ollie's a barman. He can juggle cocktail shakers like Tom Cruise.

4 Everyone at work fancies Ollie. Everyone. But the only girl he ever gave a second glance to was Eleanor.

1　Love at first sight, he often quips. She likes it when he says that. It makes her smile.

Beat. The other two stare at her like she's stupid.

2　I mean, she doesn't believe in love at first sight. She's not silly.

1　No.

2　But she likes the sentiment.

1　Yes.

2　So not love at first sight. Something better.

4　It took a while to get going though. It took Ollie two whole months to get her to go out for a drink with him.

2　She's never been that bothered about boys. It's probably why they're so crazy about her...

4　Well, she has other priorities.

2　She's one of those girls who you just know will be super successful one day. Everyone says it.

1　If Eleanor was a character in a horror film, she'd be the girl that survives.

2　She's going back to university in September. She went to university before, but the course wasn't of a high enough standard, so she dropped out. That was about a year and a half ago.

4　She's going to finish her degree at a different university, here in London. She's got her place confirmed. It's an amazing course; it's really exciting. She can't wait to be studying again.

2　She'll probably keep her job at the club though. She makes good money, and actually, she quite likes it.

4　I mean, sometimes she finds the behaviour of the other hostesses... slightly hard to bare. Film stars and famous people come in all the time, and when they do, you'll see the other girls disappear off to the bathroom one by one. They come back with shorter skirts and bigger eyes and fuller lips.

2 She doesn't judge them; she's not the judgemental type. She wishes they had more respect for themselves. But then, each to their own.

Beat.

4 I think the best thing about her, is that she's very much at peace with herself.

1 She's really worked out who she is.

2 She likes her life.

Lights flicker up on 3. *The others are disturbed by this.* 2 *clicks them down.*

They recover and are back with us , brighter than ever.

We're in the middle of an August heat wave in London. First proper Summer in years. It's a Thursday, and Ellie and Ollie both have the day off.

1 They begin the day in bed at Ollie's. He brings her breakfast; full English, which she loves –

2 *(stopping her in her tracks)* but will only have once in a blue moon.

4 There's a lido in London Fields, which is a nice twenty minute stroll from Oliver's flat. They have a lovely afternoon lounging by the pool. Occasionally one of them gets in to swim, but most of the time they sit at the side, chatting and eating overpriced food from the café.

1 They are a bit PDA –

4 but tastefully. PG rated. And then as the day begins to cool, Ollie gets a text from his friend Simon, inviting

them both to come meet him near his work for a drink.

2   Eleanor's had such a great day, that even when she realises Simon's taking them to The Duke's Hat, it doesn't really phase her.

1   Oh golly. The Duke's Hat. How to describe the Duke's Hat eh?

4   *(ignoring her)* The Duke's Hat, is what you would call a 'Fighty Lad Pub',

2   *king size.*

4   It's like the multiplex of Fighty Lad Pubs. Two whole floors of boozed-up, undirected testosterone, just begging for someone, anyone, to call it a fag so it can batter them. Ellie isn't a massive fan of the laddish type. She makes a joke as they're going in, she says

2   "Come on boys, you're all graphic design students for God's sake. How about we all just accept who we are and hop on a bus to Dalston for some craft beers?"

4   But it's a bit like showing a red rag to a bull…

2   So they go in, and it's rammed and smells a little bit like wee. It's not that Ellie's a snob; she isn't. Yes, she does like a nice candle-lit beer garden, or the option of an aubergine burger, but she'll be happy anywhere, with the right company. She makes a decision that she's going to enjoy herself anyway.

   3's lights flicker up.

3   **I'll have a San Muigel.**

   2 clicks. Lights out.

2   **I'll have an Appletiser please**

4   And eventually they find a table and the night does go well…

2   up until about nine o'clock, when Phoebe – Simon's
    girlfriend – goes to get a round in.

1   Everyone's drunk by this point,

2   apart from Eleanor. She's never been much of a drinker.

4   So Phoebe goes up to the bar and some drunken thug
    announces to the entire room that he would like to…
    uh… he'd like to do something very impolite to her.

2   And everyone laughs, all these drunken yobs standing
    around, as if there was actually some wit in that. Simon
    is on his feet immediately, and a brawl breaks out.
    Ellie wants to hide her eyes behind her hands. Ollie
    is drunkenly cheering Simon on and she wishes he
    wouldn't. But Simon's wiry little hipster-frame wasn't
    built to take much of a pounding. A couple of rounds
    of punch punch grab slap and the guy has him on the
    floor. He's kicking him and there's blood and suddenly
    the bouncers are rushing in and dragging the guy out.
    People are trying to help Simon up off the ground,
    but he's shrugging them off. His face is a state.

4   The bar manager speaks to Ellie and Ollie. The police
    have been called, part of some new initiative to reduce
    violence in the pub.

2   Yeah, good luck with that.

4   He wants them to make a statement, but they just want
    to get out of there, so they leave their details and make
    a move. Outside, Phoebe's trying to hail a cab for her
    and Simon. He's giving her the cold shoulder.

1   Poor girl.

2   Ellie and Ollie get a night bus home. And on the way
    back, they agree that although the end of the night
    was a bit tense, it didn't ruin the day. And –

    They receive a text message. Ignore it.

    And –

They receive a text message. Ignore it.

And –

They receive a text message. Give in. **2** *gets her phone out. They read. Long pause. It's devastating but they try not to let it show. Back to us with brighter smiles than ever. In the back,* **3***'s light is flickering like crazy.*

Ellie's had an idea!

4 She thinks she might go on holiday!

2 Well, not even a holiday, she thinks she might go travelling.

4 She's never been travelling, and it's one of those things you really should do.

1 Asia maybe. Or South America.

4 She'd love to see those ruins in Peru.

2 And here's the funny thing;

They all find it funny.

She might not tell anyone she's going!

4 She might just go!

1 Just to be quirky and adventurous!

2 has noticed that **3***'s light is on. She tries to click it out, but it isn't working. Frantically, she keeps trying as the others continue.*

4 Just to have that story, to say she did that in her life!

1 Just because she was so wild at heart and couldn't be in the city any more and it was all so spur of the moment

4 Just because

1 Just because

3 Because she's dug herself into a really deep hole and now she can't see any way –

> *Desperately,* **2** *pulls the plug out of the wall on the* **3***'s light, and it goes out, cutting her off. She returns to the centre of the stage. She looks like she might burst into tears. She holds it together, and continues.*

2 She could go teach English in Tibet! She could go for a whole year! Maybe she'd find herself out there, find a life that she really loved, and never come back! Who knows? It's such a great idea she can't believe she never thought of it before. She goes online and starts looking up plane prices.

> *Unbeknownst to* **2***,* **3***'s light is back on.*

She could go in a few days. She could –

3 She's been receiving these text messages.

> *Beat.* **2** *doesn't know what to do. She decides to pretend it isn't happening.*

2 She's –

3 She's been receiving these text messages from a number she doesn't know.

> *Beat.*

2 And she thinks she might just delete them. She tried calling it, but no one picked up. So…

> **2** *gets her phone out and goes to delete them, but* **3** *snatches the phone from her.*

3 The text messages read:

> "Hello Scarlet."
> "I saw you in the pub tonight. Is your friend okay?"
> "Why do they call you Eleanor?"
> "Has your boyfriend seen the video?"

"I think I might send it to him. Is his name Oliver Coen?"

2 *grabs the phone back.*

1 She hasn't responded to any of them. Her councillor told her –

2 *makes an angry/horrified noise, cutting her off.*

Sorry.

Beat.

A... mental health professional... that she knew... told her, in passing, that bullies feed on your negative energy, and you shouldn't indulge them. And now she's deleted them.

2 She knows who's sending them. Eleanor changed her number before she left uni, so there's only one person it could be.

3 Daniel.

They shoot her an annoyed look.

4 Yes, Daniel. Daniel was Eleanor's first boyfriend. She was utterly besotted with him. Then one day she came home and found him in bed with her best friend, so she dumped him.

3 No.

4 Yes.

3 No.

4 *(suddenly angry)* Yes. Yes yes yes. Shush.

Beat. 4 *takes a moment to cool down, regain control.*

She was completely heartbroken. It took her a long time to trust any one again. But then she found Oliver and everything was better than ever.

2 But that's life isn't it. You meet someone when you're young and you're absolutely obsessed with each other, but it can't last forever. It's all just a part of you becoming the person you're going to be.

Beat.

4 She really thinks travelling could be the best decision she's ever –

3 *has her phone to her ear.*

3 **Hi, Sasha, it's me.**

The others are horrified.

Yeah I know, I'm so sorry; I've been awful. Listen, I can't chat for –

2 *snatches the phone from her and hijacks the conversation.*

2 **Hi, Sasha! It's me!**

She lets out a little scream of excitement!

I know I know, it's been too long! We *must* do something about that! How are you?

Beat.

Oh you know: busy busy! *(she giggles).* **Listen, I can't chat for long, I need a favour. I'm looking for Daniel, but his old number doesn't work anymore. Do you know what he's doing these days?**

Beat.

No darling, I don't have Facebook. Could you look it up for me?

The next response shocks her.

London? You're sure? London?

3 Told you.

> *Beat.* 1 *and* 4 *hand* 2 *paper and pen and she writes the next bit down:*

2 **Cranston... Charter... Inter... national... Okay. Thank you so much. You know, you must come down some time! Ok! Ok bye now! Ciao!**

4 From her dear old friend Sasha, Eleanor discovers that Daniel is working as an intern at a big financial company. In London.

2 There's only one thing for it: she's going to have to go see him.

4 Oh no, she isn't is she? Poor guy, he's obviously still in love with her. When Eleanor dumped him, it was... well, he hounded her with phone calls and text messages for months, turned up drunk on her doorstep night after night begging her to take him back. It was a mess, an absolute mess.

2 She's going to be gentle, but firm.

4 She needs to make him accept that it's over between them, no matter how much he wants her back. And as for this so-called 'video'...

2 Well, Eleanor doesn't know anything about any 'video'.

4 She has no idea what he's talking about, but whatever it is she's going to put a stop to it.

2 She's going to put a stop to it, even though she's almost one-hundred percent certain that it doesn't exist and he's made it up. Whatever it is.

3 *coughs. She is getting frustrated.*

3 Cranston Charter International.

Annoyance from **2** *and* **4**. *They give some air before they continue; they don't want* **3** *to think she's in charge.*

2 Cranston Charter International is housed within a massive glass skyscraper, right in the heart of the City. Out the front there is a courtyard, with greenery and a fountain and lots of pigeons. She arrives at about four. Obviously way too early, but she has no way of knowing what time Daniel will finish, and she doesn't want to drag this out.

Her phone starts to ring.

3 Ollie calls at ten past five.

4 And the thing is, she *could* tell him where she was, but boys can be so sensitive, and why should it matter?

2 "Hi hun, can't really talk right now, I'm helping Mum out at the gallery."

3 Her mind has become so quick, so well-oiled,

2 "I mean I could maybe come over later, but you never know with this. There's so much paperwork, and she's so stressed at the moment."

3 that she barely even has to think about the lies.

1 And then she spots him, making his way through the swirly doors; Daniel.

A collective gasp. She ends the phone call mid-conversation.

1 He isn't alone, Daniel. He's hand in hand with a girl. Laughing. Swinging arms. Like a poster.

Pause. They are obviously more affected by this than they thought they would be.

4 She's beautiful, this girl. Disney princess beautiful.

   She realises what she has said. **2** *gives her evils.*

   But Eleanor, she's relieved, because, because, it doesn't,
   y'know, it's… she's…

   *Pause. It's a punch on the heart. They are all united in
   this, but* **4** *feels it particularly harshly.* **3** *doesn't allow it
   to atrophy her for too long.*

3 They're almost out of sight and she hasn't even got up.

   None of the others move.

   They're almost out of sight and she hasn't even got up!

   Beat.

   She runs. She runs to catch up with them and once
   they're firmly within her sights she slows to a walk;
   head down, hood up. Through the streets, down into
   the underground, one tube, two tubes, all the time
   trying to gee herself up to confront him, but just, she
   will in a minute, she will in a minute,

4 She um, she doesn't want to… because it would be
   unfair on him, with his new, new… it would be wrong
   to confuse him like that.

   Beat. **4** *is distraught.*

3 She nearly loses them three times. At Stockwell the girl
   gets off. They share a sweet, polite kiss, and as the train
   sets off he watches her disappear down the platform.
   At Clapham Common, he gets off. And Eleanor
   follows, up and out, through streets and streets. On a
   particularly leafy suburban road, buried in the depths
   of a whole host of other leafy, suburban roads, Daniel
   reaches a house. And goes in.

   They stare at the house. It's a nice house.

She wonders how he can afford to live in a place like this while interning. His dad works for JP Morgan; she doesn't spend too long puzzling it out.

1 And then...

3 And then it just kind of slows to a halt.

2 *(accusatory, to* 3*)* Because she doesn't actually *have a plan.*

3 *(giving every bit of attitude back)* But she's *working on it.*

4 *(panicking)* One-way flights from London to Thailand: £342.90. One way flights from London to Sydney –

3 Shut up!

2 *is not impressed by this.*

Sorry. I'm trying to think.

2 Because that's worked out so well for us in the past.

3 Would you like to have a go? No seriously, if you have an idea, I'm more than happy to let you take over.

2 Well it's not this, that's for certain.

3 So that's a no then?

2 If it weren't for you, we wouldn't be in this mess in the first place!

3 So get us out of it, if you're so clever. Give us a plan. *Anything* apart from "bury your head in the sand".

Beat.

2 We all agreed that we weren't doing things your way anym –

3 I'm still not hearing any suggestions.

2 We all agreed. The three of us. We don't want you –

3 What, they can't speak for themselves?

2 Fine. You're right. If you want to go with her, feel free.

All attention is on the two subordinates. They are silent, cowed, two children stuck between warring parents.

I didn't think so.

3 I didn't hear them say anything.

2 Because they feel bad for you.

3 We are up shit creek and I seem to be the only one who's willing to get dirty.

2 Exactly. We don't want to be dirty anymore. That's why we got rid of you.

Ouch. Pause.

3 Look, this is not a coup. Just give me a chance to sort this out, for all of us. And then when I'm done, I promise you I will return to my corner and you can all go back to pretending none of it ever happened.

Beat.

1 I…

2 What?

Beat.

1 I think we should give it a try.

2 No you don't.

1 Just a short one. Just to see.

Beat. 2 *wasn't expecting this.*

2 Well, maybe we don't care what you think. *(to 4)* Right?

Silence from 4.

Right?

4 *shrugs.*

What does that mean?

Beat.

4 *looks at the ground.*

Beat.

2 You can't be serious.

4 *won't meet her eye.*

Pause. A defeat.

Wow.

Beat.

Fine. Okay. But when it's done, you are gone. And if this goes tits-up, I want everyone to remember I objected. Come on.

2, *starts to move to the edge of the space.*

4 *follows.*

1 *stays, looks longingly at* **3**.

2 *(to* **1***)* Come on.

1 *follows.*

3 *is left on her own.*

The floor is yours.

3 Right. Okay. Daniel's house. Okay. Okay…

She composes herself.

It's about an hour later, when Dan leaves the house again, that I know what I'm going to–

2 She.

3 Excuse me?

2 She. Eleanor. It's about an hour later, when Dan leaves the house again, that *she* knows what *she's* going to... blah blah blah.

3 No.

2 No?

3 You said I could do it my way. This is my way.

She recomposes.

It's about an hour later, when Dan leaves the house again, that I know how I'm going to play it. I wait until he's around the corner, and then approach the front door.

She rings the bell.

The girl who answers is small, with big glasses; she slightly brings to mind that one out of The Chipmunks.

Hi, I'm here to see Daniel?

She stares at me like I'm an alien.

GIRL **Ehm... sorry, I don't think he's in at the moment. Ehm... do you want to leave a message, or anything?**

No, that's okay. I work with him at Cranston Charter. He said I should just wait for him in his room?

The girl doesn't seem sure.

Fucking homework, know what I mean?

GIRL *(unconvinced)* **Aye. Right.**

Beat.

So, can I come in?

GIRL **Yeah. Sure. Sorry.**

She moves out of the way and I step inside.

GIRL **Second left at the top.**

I'm halfway up the stairs when she speaks again.

GIRL **Ehm…**

I turn back. She hasn't moved.

Sorry, did you say something?

GIRL **Ehm… no. No nothing. Never mind.**

She goes to **DANIEL** *'s room.*

Dan's room hasn't changed. At all. Same colours. Same posters. Same smell… A cardigan I bought him the first birthday we were together is hanging over the edges of the wash-basket. On his desk, the copy of American Psycho I never got back is looking very well used.

I feel a bit like a ghost. It's fucking weird.

She moves on.

His laptop is on his desk. I pick it up and position myself on the bed. I open up the laptop and switch it on; the log in screen appears, complete with familiar wallpaper. I enter his password…

She types in a password. Beat.

I enter his password…

She types in a password. Beat.

Wait. Hang on. Um.

She types in a password.

She types it again.

She types it again.

Shit. Okay. There's a problem. He *may* have changed it.

She starts typing manically.

I try the names of other Cardiff rugby players I know. Then Welsh nationals, Chelsea football players, GTA characters, Holly Willoughby's birthday. In a moment of desperate panic I consider just taking the laptop and doing a runner. And that's when I hear someone outside the door.

She freezes. Slowly, she closes the laptop and puts it back on the desk.

She watches the door, tense, then

Dan?

Nothing happens. She continues to stare, frozen.

The door opens, and in steps the girl from downstairs. I let out a breath I wasn't even aware I was holding.

GIRL **Hi.**

she says

Hello I return, very casual.

Silence.

... You ok?

GIRL **Ehm...**

Beat.

GIRL **I know this is probably none of my business, so please stop me if I'm overstepping the mark, but...**

Girl considers her words.

GIRL **Don't do this to yourself.**

Excuse me?

GIRL Dan has a girlfriend. I don't know what he's told you, but he isn't going to leave her. He just isn't.

Um... sorry... um... I think you may have got the wrong idea. I'm just... I'm just a work colleague.

GIRL I know who you are.

2 What?

3/GIRL I don't think you remember me... I was at uni with you. Jenny? I was a friend of Amanda's?

2 Hang on.

3/GIRL Scarlet, right?

2 No, Eleanor.

3 ... is what I'm trying to say, but my mouth has gone dry.

2 No. No.

3 ... is all I can muster, my tongue tripping over itself in denial.

GIRL That's why I had to come say something; I think it's awful, what happened to you.

2 Okay, time out.

3/GIRL I have a friend who went through a very similar thing, and it really messed her up.

2 /I said time out! HEY.

3/GIRL She did a lot of things she ended up regretting.

2 *(screaming at the other two)* What are you doing!?

3/GIRL You don't have to make /yourself that girl.

2 She's doing it again I told /you I told you she would!

3 Short sharp breaths./ I can't feel my arms.

2 Please, please stop!/ You promised!

3 All I can hear is the/ blood pounding in my ears.

2 /STOP. STOP IT.

3 My heart is at one hundred beats per second and all I
   want her to do is –

2 SHUT UP.

   2 *slaps* 3. *Hard.*

   Silence. 3 *recovers herself, and looks* 2 *right in the eye.*
   (A victory?)

3 I don't know what happens. I'm on my feet, and I've
   slapped her. Hard.

2 *(horrified)* What? No!

3/GIRL **What the fuck? Are you fucking crazy?**

2 No, that's not how it/ works!

3/GIRL **I'm trying to help you, you/ psycho bitch.**

2 You can't do that!

   3 *pushes* 2. 2 *hits her.*

3 She pushes me back. I hit –

   2 *puts her hand over* 3*'s mouth; she tries to talk but
   can't.* 1 *speaks up.*

1 I've got one hand over her mouth and the other around
   her neck.

   2 *spins her head around to* 1, *shocked and betrayed.*

   She bites down hard on me.

   3 *bites* 2*'s hand. She lets out a horrible cry and releases
   her grip. Everyone goes silent.*

   2 *has a breakdown. They watch. She storms off stage/she
   storms off to the corner.*

2 FUCK OFF.

She slams the door behind her/3 clicks the light out in
2's corner.

Long silence. 3 and 1 meet eyes. A pact is made…

…and suddenly they're back in the action.

1 All hell breaks loose. She's screaming and I'm screaming
and she's pulling me towards the door and at some
point I kick her really hard in the shin and she lets
out this horrible high-pitched whine. Two guys appear
and they're basically carrying me out of the house and
I'm kicking and shouting and hugging the laptop to
my chest, and she's crying and I think at some point
I tell her that if she ever touches me again I will kill
her. Meters away from the front door I manage to gain
the upper hand by elbowing one of them right in the
stomach. I make a break for freedom, laptop tucked
under one elbow, they're right at my heels, I fling the
door open and…

Daniel is standing on the doorstep. Everything halts.
He stares at me, confused. I think I might have split
my lip.

3 Oh fuck. Oh fuck. Oh fuck oh fuck.

1 **Hello.** I say.

–

1 If I'm being honest, I imagine a reunion with Dan most
days. These fantasies come in various forms, from the
tragically predictable to the worryingly bizarre. My
councillor calls this 'a cycle of self-loathing'.

None of my imaginings have ever involved me breaking
into his house and beating up one of his friends.

Beat.

I'm sat alone in his room for about twenty minutes while they all talk downstairs. I'm not sure what about. Maybe it's just a ploy to keep me here while they call the police. Or the social services.

3   And then he appears; The Responsible Adult.

  1 *becomes* **DANIEL**..

1/DANIEL   **Ok. All right. What's going on?**

  Silence.

  They all think I should call the police. Is that what I should do?

3   **No.**

1/DANIEL   **What the fuck Scarlet? I mean, where do I start? What were you doing with my computer?**

3   **I… thought…**

1/DANIEL   **You thought what?**

  SCARLET *shows* **DANIEL** *the text messages on her phone.*

3   **Is this you?**

1/DANIEL   **What is this?**

  I explain the situation.

  DANIEL *is reading the texts.*

1/DANIEL   **I didn't send these.**

3   **Of everyone in Manchester, only you and Sasha had this number.**

1/DANIEL   **Then try her.**

3   **I don't believe you.**

1/DANIEL   **Really not my problem.**

3   **Dan, I'm not here to have a go at you –**

1/DANIEL Ha! Are you taking the piss? Have a go at ME?

3 What I mean is, I'm not here to cause a fuss and yes before you say anything I am aware that I already caused a fuss but what I'm saying is I just want to resolve this and then I'll leave you alone.

1/DANIEL Well, great, it's resolved. Off you pop.

SCARLET *isn't having it.*

1/DANIEL Scarlet, why would I do something like this? Why would I bother?

3 Because.

1/DANIEL Because what?

3 I put those pictures of you up.

1/DANIEL So?

3 I'm really sorry. I did it in a – I was very hurt by what you did. I took them down as soon as I –

1/DANIEL Scarlet. Who cares? I didn't. It was a laugh, a bit of banter with my mates. I actually had a few girls come up to me, who'd seen them.

3 But –

1/DANIEL People didn't like you as much as you thought they did.

3 At this point, his phone starts to ring.

DANIEL *picks up.*

1/DANIEL Hi, can I call you back? Someone's here.

No, no one, no one you know. I'll tell you about it later.

He hangs up.

1/DANIEL Right. You gotta go.

3 Show me your laptop.

1/DANIEL Scuse me?

3 I just need to know it's not on there..

1/DANIEL I'm sorry, are you under the impression that I owe you something?

3 Dan, please, I need some help.

1/DANIEL Look at yourself. You're a mess mate. This ain't normal Scarlet; it's fucking weird.

3 I know.

1/DANIEL It's time to move on. I did, a long time ago.

Long pause. SCARLET *is embarrassed.*

Ok, this is making me feel really uncomfortable. Here's a deal; promise me that I will never see you again, and you can look on my computer. How's that?

Beat.

3 Yeah.

1/DANIEL Promise me?

3 Yes.

1/DANIEL No, promise me. I want to hear the words.

3 I promise.

Dan gives me free reign to search around his computer. Much to his annoyance, I take that and run with it. I spend forty-five minutes checking every video on his hard drive. The volume of porn is… disconcerting… but my video isn't to be found. Which means… back to square one.

Beat.

1 Having finished, he shows me to the door. Our goodbye is abrupt, and wordless. It's only as he shuts the door behind me that I realise I still had something

important to say. But it's too late. I turn back and stare at the door. The one last thing I would have said to Dan, if I'd had the chance, was:

4   "You were awful to me."

   1 *and* 3 *turn to* 4.

   Beat.

   Isn't it funny; I've only just figured that out.

   Pause. 4 *has made a realisation. A moment between the three of them, and then she rejoins.*

   I walk the whole way home.

   –

4   It's a staring-at-the-ceiling kind of an evening. I have no idea what to do next. There are no leads left to follow. I sit on my bed and half-watch an episode of Murder She Wrote, wondering what Jessica Fletcher would do in my situation. Which leaves me wondering what a Jessica Fletcher sex tape would actually be like…

1   It's a disturbing thought.

4   At eight o'clock, Ollie calls, but I don't pick up. I don't know what I'd say to him. It'd just be another knot in the tangle.

1   Another Jenga block to pull out of the tower.

4   At nine o'clock he calls again, and this time he leaves a message.

3/OLLIE   **El, what's going on? I know you're not at the gallery. Come on, you said you wouldn't do this anymore. I can't keep…**

   Beat.

   You know what, I don't want to do this on your voicemail. Just call me. If I don't hear from you before

I go to bed, I think we need to have a serious chat about... well, about us, and this relationship.

4 This happens sometimes. I go off the grid for a few days, don't talk to anyone, take some time out to spend with my duvet. He usually deals with it quite well, bless him, but every so often I'll get a message like this. Sometimes I get so annoyed. I want to scream at him "Why are you letting me treat you like this? I'm a fucking bitch! Just end it!"

1 But not today. Today I just feel bad. So I go onto Buzzfeed and scroll through 48 Life-Changing Quesedillas You Need To Know About. Then I play some Fruit Ninja. Then I –

The sound of an incoming text message

At ten o'clock I receive another text from my mystery tormentor.

She gets out her phone and reads it.

"Hello Scarlet. Is this your boyfriend's number?"

4 Underneath is pasted a phone number. It's Ollie's.

1 I think I might give him a call tonight, fill him in on a few things.

4 My stomach clenches. I feel sick.

Beat.

1 This time, I text back.

She types out a message.

4 Don't do this. Please don't do this.

1 "What... do... you... want... from... me?"

4 I am begging you.

1   I put the phone down try not to think about it. Five
    minutes feel like an hour.

    Sound of an incoming text. She picks the phone back up.

    It says

4   "I want to see you."

    Beat.

    The sound of another incoming text. She reads.

    Beat.

1   It's an address.

    —

3   It's just after midnight when I arrive; a darkened
    high-rise just off the Walworth Road. I'd imagined
    something a bit more well lit, and on street level;
    somewhere I could ring the doorbell and then stand
    back behind a gate. This is a bad idea; I know that,
    I do, but what choice do I have? The one thing that
    scares me more than coming here, is the thought of
    what might happen if I don't.

    At the door I buzz the intercom and wait. Someone
    picks up, but nothing is said; crackling, and then the
    door clicks open. In the lift, I punch in the top floor
    and when the doors reopen I step out onto a long,
    dark balcony. London's lights stretch out way below
    me. It's almost silent. Even the cars sound a million
    miles away.

    Lights up on **2**, *darkness everywhere else.*

    *She is completely alone. She walks along the balcony,
    and arrives at a door.*

    She gathers her nerves, and rings the bell.

Pause.

WILL *answers.*

4/WILL **All right?**

2 **...**

4/WILL **You wanna come in?**

2 **...**

4/WILL **Not a great idea, girl like you standing out there at this time of night.**

2 **...**

4/WILL **Look, you can come in or you can go home.**

Beat.

2 **Ok.**

She steps inside. He closes the door and they are in the entry hall.

4/WILL **Lemme take your coat.**

She takes it off and gives it to him.

My room's at the end.

This is a grim fact, and she takes it in.
He herds her up the corridor.
They go to his room.
She moves as far from him as possible
Awkward silence.

4/WILL **So.**

How you been?

2 **Fine.**

Last twenty four hours have been a bit rough.

4/WILL It's nice to see you.

You look good. I like your hair like that. It's better.

Pause.

You still see any of the old lot? Like, from uni and that?

2 No, not really.

4/WILL What about your little friend? What was her name? Looked like a troll?

2 Sasha.

4/WILL She used to make me laugh. You see her?

2 No. Not for a while.

4/WILL Funny how quickly you leave it all behind.

Pause.

Can I get you a drink?

2 *shakes her head.*

Glass of wine?

2 No.

4/WILL I got a job in a pub; been learning a lot about wine. Never really saw myself as wine man, but...

2 The Duke's Hat?

4/WILL Yeah.

2 Is that where you work?

4/WILL You didn't see me did you.

2 ...

4/WILL I wanted to say hello, but we were rammed. And then your mate got into that fight, and you all left your numbers on the contact sheet...

2 ...

4/WILL Everyone at work thinks you're really fit.

2 ...

4/WILL I'm gonna get a drink. Make yourself at home.

> *He leaves.*
>
> **SCARLET** *does her breathing exercises; in for five, out for five, in for five, out for five. They aren't working.*
>
> **WILL** *reappears with a glass of wine.*
>
> *They watch each other.*
>
> *He takes a sip.*
>
> *He approaches her, awkwardly.*
>
> *He touches her. She can't look him in the eye.*
>
> *He kisses her. It takes a second, but she pulls away.*
>
> *He tries to kiss her again, but she turns her head.*

2 Stop.

> *Pause.*

4/WILL Take your top off.

2 Please Will. Please.

4/WILL Take it off.

2 I can't.

4/WILL Scarlet.

2 I am so sorry for anything/ I ever did to you.

4/WILL Hey. Shhh. Hey.

2 I am begging you. I will do anything else I will –

> *He has his phone out. The video is playing. It stops her.*
>
> *She watches the video in horrified silence.*
>
> *He stops it. Puts his phone away.*
>
> *He watches her.*

She is almost broken.

She takes the wine from him and downs the whole glass.

He sits down on the bed. Indicates for her to join him.

She can't.

She does.

He rubs her thigh.

She buries her head in her hands.

4/WILL **Hey. Don't cry. Come on. Don't cry.**

This isn't how he wanted or imagined it.

Let me get you another drink.

He leaves.

She is alone with her thoughts.

She makes the hardest decision she's ever had to make.

Lights up everywhere. The other three **SCARLET**s *are here, watching the fourth.*

1 There was a time –

3 If I'm being completely honest –

1 there was a time when I would have done anything to make that video disappear.

4 Anything.

1 And I know that sounds terrible, I know it does…

4 but it's the truth.

3 I would have stayed here.

Beat.

2 But not anymore. There is nothing in the world I want that much. It's over.

We're back in the room. But now **2** *is joined by the rest of them; reunited.*

4   I'm on my feet and at the threshold.

2   Peering around the corner, I can see Will in the kitchen.

1   uncorking a bottle,

3   back turned.

1   There isn't much time.

2   I make a silent dash for the door, grab the latch and…

They're at the door. **2** *reaches for the latch…*

And…

4   What's wrong?

2   It won't open.

1   What?

2   I pull at the door, once, twice, three times, thinking it's stuck, trying desperately not to make any noise, attract his attention,

3   only to realise…

2   It's locked. The door's locked. He's locked the door.

A moment of horror-struck realisation.

1   It's a cold sweat moment, time momentarily stops…

3   and I realise that I have absolutely fucked up.

4   Abort! Abort! Turn back!

2   I can't move.

1   Get back in there!

2   My thoughts are moving so much faster than anything else.

4/WILL **Scarlet?**

She spins around, terrified.

Were you leaving?

1 **What?**

No.

No, I just needed some air. That all got a bit intense didn't it.

WILL *says nothing. His silence in intimidating.*

(smiley, casually) **You've locked the door.**

4/WILL **Bit cheeky, you trying to creep out like that.**

1 **Just felt a bit faint.**

4/WILL **Let's go back in there.**

He approaches her.

1 **I just want to get some air.**

He hands her the wine.

4/WILL **Come on.**

1 **Let me out.**

He grabs her wrist and starts to pull her.

She smashes the wine glass over his head.

3 I run.

2 I'm on the stairs and he's right behind me. He grabs my leg and pulls and I just about manage to grab onto a bannister. I'm screaming

1 **HELP! HELP!**

2 praying that someone somewhere can hear me, kicking out with my leg frantically

1 **STOP IT STOP PLEASE!**

3 My foot connects with his face and he falls back down
   the stairs. My stomach hits the edge of a step, and I am
   winded.

2 I'm back on my feet and I'm pounding up the stairs and
   somehow he is only just behind me

1 I'm flying into the toilet and throwing my weight back
   on the door just as he slams into it. He falls back and I
   throw the latch across.

   They collapse back. **WILL** *bangs on the door and screams
   unintelligibly.*

2 It's a tiny, tiny room. Just a toilet. Not even a sink. There's
   a window above the toilet and I climb up to it hastily.

1 It opens.

3 Outside is a hundred foot drop. Nothing else.

1 He can kick that door in. Easy.

   He rages at the door again.

2 **Will! Please! Stop!**

   He kicks the door.

1 **I'm so sorry. I'm so sorry. It was an accident.**

4/WILL **BITCH!**

2 Call the police.

3 I reach into my bag for my phone…

1 My bag. My bag!

3 Where…

2 I scramble around looking for it, but it's not here.

3 I must have dropped it in the struggle.

1   *(Almost hyperventilating, searching around frantically)* No.
No no no no no no no no no. No. It has to – No.

4/WILL   You have five seconds to open that door or I swear
to God I will kick it in. And then I will be fucking livid.

3   Ok, calm down.

4/WILL   OPEN THE FUCKING DOOR.

   1 *starts crying afresh.*

4/WILL   Oh of course, cos you're the fucking victim aren't
you.

2   Please, please Will. Please.

4/WILL   Not so funny now am I?

3   I never laughed at you. I never found you funny.

   *He kicks and bangs and rages at the door with everything
   it has. The* SCARLET*s try to keep the door intact.*

   He has tired himself out.

   Silence. Heavy breathing.

4/WILL   You're a bitch.

   Silence. Heavy breathing.

   You fucking fucked it up for me.

3   I never meant for any of that to happen.

4/WILL   No of course you didn't. I saw you and your little
mate smirking at me. You thought you were hilarious.

3   That's not true.

4/WILL   I never lived that down. No one ever let it go. Not
that anyone liked me before, but...

3   Someone asked me if I'd slept with you. I just told the
truth.

4/WILL I couldn't tell them that you'd blown me off; *you*, the fucking bike of Manchester.

3 That's not my fault.

Silence.

4/WILL Why am I so disgusting to you?

3 You're not.

2 You are. You fucking –

    1 *puts her hand over 2's mouth to stop her.*

1 You're not.

4/WILL We had a drink. We had a laugh.

Pause.

Come out.

3 I can't.

4/WILL Please come out.

3 I can't do that.

    WILL *rages and kicks the door, but it is weaker.*

Will, I'm calling the police, ok?

He doesn't respond.

I'm calling them now.

1 I dial 999 in my mind and wait. "Police" I tell the imaginary officer. I give my name, and I explain the situation. I give the address. I thank the kind police woman, and hang up.

2 Will?

4 He doesn't respond.

2 Will? They're coming.

4 Nothing.

   Pause.

3 I don't really know what to do next.

   Long silence.

2 Half an hour later, I open the door. Will is gone. Or
   he's hiding. I go downstairs and pick up my bag. The
   door's hanging wide open. I leave.

4 Upon reaching the main road, I exhale. I've been
   holding my breath since I opened the toilet door. And
   yet, I feel...

1 Calm?

3 Rational.

4 'Men are afraid that women will laugh at them. Women
   are afraid that men will kill them.'

1 It's a quote I remember from somewhere.

4 I can't stop thinking about it, in this really cold, really
   analytical kind of a way. I'm literally just playing it over
   and over in my mind.

2 I wonder if this means I'm in shock. Is this what shock is?

   She ponders.

3 I take all these thoughts and feelings and push them to
   the back of the queue. There will be plenty of time for
   them tomorrow. For now, I fear the night is not yet
   finished.

2 Before taking a step forward, I allow myself one last look
   back; the tower block half obscured from view...

1 I hope that I never have to see Will again in my life. I
   don't know what I'd do if I did.

3 I'm booking myself into some karate lessons first thing in the morning, that's for fucking sure.

4 But there's a very real part of me, in this odd moment of stillness I'm having, that wonders... what will become of him?

    –

1 The cab ride plays out like an ending sequence. Staring out the window as the city slides by; The Shard, The Gherkin, empty offices with the lights left on. I allow myself to entertain the big questions: Who am I? Where am I? etc. Eleanor is no more; what does that mean for the people that made up her life? They don't feel like they belong to me.

3 A memory:

1 stepping off a train at St Pancras, still, still drunk, and falling into a cab much like this one.

4 Arriving back at to an empty home. Hiding in my room for a week, telling Mum I had the flu, which is kind of what it felt like.

2 My advisor at the Job Centre, her name was Temperance; I asked her to call me Eleanor, and I remember thinking it was such a good idea, such a great step towards a fresh start.

3 The cab pulls up outside a flat in Bethnal Green. Silently I pay up. Climb out. And then; I'm standing outside Ollie's front door. The knot in my stomach has it's own heartbeat.

4 Another memory:

1 Daniel's doorstep, one o'clock in the morning; drunk off my face and screaming his name.

2 Breathe in. Breathe out.

    She rings the doorbell.

Beat.

3 I'm inside the house.

4 Ollie is offering me food; halloumi curry, which is weirdly the only thing he knows how to make. He's still angry, but he's dealing with it well. Ollie is someone who softens quickly. I find myself thinking that I would like for us to have a chance to get to know one another properly. I hope this isn't the end of that.

1 I'm in Ollie's room, sitting on his bed. He's downstairs making up a bowl. I'm concentrating on my breathing. In for five, out for five, in for five, out for five. It's a habit that I employ almost without thinking now. So many times, wide awake in the dead of night.

3 A final memory:

2 Sasha's room, sat on her bed. I'm distraught. She's comforting me. She tells me that I should have been wiser. I should have been careful. I should have kept my legs closed. That, really, it's all my fault. And something horrible happened in that moment; quietly, at the back of my mind, a switch was flipped. And I believed her.

1 I am a girl who has had a fair amount of sex for my years,

2 with a fair amount of men,

3 and one woman.

4 I am lucky, in that

1 I pretty much always enjoyed myself,

3 even with the shit ones.

4 And that's a good thing. I think that should be celebrated,

2 not punished.

1 Ollie is standing in front of me, holding out a bowl of home-made curry. It might be a peace offering. I take it, place it to one side. My appetite has been put on hold, but I'm optimistic that it will come back later. He's sat on the bed beside me. There's silence. I am calm.

4 I turn to him. Eyes meet.

3 Finally, I am ready to tell my story.

   Beat.

2 And so I do.

The End

Property List

ACT 1

At a barbecue (p3)
Sofa (p5)
The scene comes apart (p5)
Student Union bar area (p6)
Pint (p6)
Pint (p6)
Scarlet gathers her stuff (p7)
Scarlet's coat (p7)
Sandwich (p8)
Sainsbury's bag with lunch in (p8)
Scarlet's two mobile phones (p9)
Shots (p11)
Scarlet's room (p11)
Video filmed on a camera phone (p12)
Will's room (p14)
Cake ingredients (p22)
Big mixing bowl (p23)
Wooden spoon to mix (p23)
Whipped cream (p23)
Picnic hamper (p24)
Baby oil (p24)
Flapjack bites (p24)
Candles (p24)
Funny hand-made card (p24)
Birthday present (p24)
Bed (p26)
Exam room (p28)
Table (p28)
Chair (p28)
Exam paper (p29)
Big bottle of vodka (p29)
Suitcase (p33)
Mobile phone (p33)

ACT 2

Costume: All Scarlets dressed in Conservative clothes, hair and make-up (p35)

Mobile phone (p35)
Pen (p44)
Paper (44)
Outside Daniel's house (p46)
Daniel's bedroom (p51)
Laptop (p51)
Walks along a balcony and reaches a door (p61)
Entry hall (p62)
Will's bedroom (p63)
Glass of wine (p64)
Will's mobile phone (p64)

Lighting List

ACT 1

Dark, illuminated solely by the light of the television (p5)
Lights up (p11)
Light spills in (p29)
Blackout (p34)

ACT 2

Dark corner (p35)
Lights flicker up on 3, but 2 clicks them down (p37)
3's light flickers up (p38)
2 clicks lights down (p38)
Lights flicker like crazy (p40)
2 tries to click 3's light of (p40)
2 pulls the plug off the wall to turn 3's light off (p41)
3's light is back on (p41)
3 clicks the light out in 2's corner (p55)
Lights up on 2, but darkness everywhere else (p61)
Lights up everywhere (p65)

Sound Effects List

ACT 1

Knock at the door (p10)
Video being played (p12)
Phone rings (p15)
Phone rings (p15)
Phone rings (p16)
Phone rings (p20)
Scarlet knocks (p24)
Clock ticking (p28)
Two shushes – all of the voices (p29)
Front door opens (p29)

ACT 2

Phone rings (p45)
Rings doorbell (p50)
Slams the door (p55)
Sound of an incoming text message (p60)
Sound of an incoming text message (p60)
Sound of another incoming text message (p61)
Video playing from phone (p64)
Will bangs on the door (p68)
Rings the doorbell at Ollie's (p72)

Lightning Source UK Ltd.
Milton Keynes UK
UKOW06f0611100415

249390UK00001B/5/P